MY VISION FROM PRISON

POETIC THOUGHTS

BY

VINCENT GAMBOA-HIGINIO

To order additional copies of this book, contact:
Xlibris
844-714-8691
www.Xlibris.com
Orders@Xlibris.com

ISBN: Softcover   978-1-6698-1752-9
        EBook   978-1-6698-1751-2

Print information available on the last page

Rev. date: 03/24/2022

TABLE OF CONTENTS

OPENING PRAYER

DEAR DIVINE CREATOR, PLEASE GUIDE OUR SPIRITS TO UNDERSTAND YOUR KNOWLEDGE AND WALK WITH YOUR WISDOM. BE THE LIGHT THAT GUIDES OUR STEPS AND BLESS US WITH YOUR TENDER LOVING CARE.

O BELOVED CREATOR, YOU HAVE CREATED US TO CREATIVELY CREATE OUR OWN CREATION AND YOUR LIGHT IS THE ENERGY THAT MAKES US SHINE.

PLEASE HUMBLE THE SPIRIT YOU HAVE PLACED WITHIN US AND MAKE US ONE AGAIN.

GUIDE US TO UNDERSTAND THE POWER IN THE ENERGY OF YOUR LIGHT.

GUIDE US TO VALUE THE TRUTH IN THE WORDS WE UTTER AND TO DISCERN FALSEHOOD IN OTHERS WHEN WE HEAR THEM.

TEACH US TO BUILD A SOLID FOUNDATION OF TRUTH AND LOVE WHEREVER WE GO WITH WISDOM, UNDERSTANDING AND PERSEVERANCE AS THE PRINCIPLES FROM WHICH WE BUILD.

ENERGY WE BE

WE ARE ALL IN THE PROCESS OF A DIVINE CREATION, YAH HAS CREATED US NOT TO BE SEPARATED FROM THE ENERGY OF CREATION BUT TO BE AT ONENESS WITH THIS DIVINE ENERGY. YAH, JAH, ALLAH, GOD, THE CHRIST, BUDDHA, BY WHATEVER NAME YOU WANT TO CALL THIS AWESOME ENERGY DID IN FACT CREATE US TO CREATIVELY CREATE CREATION. THIS POWERFUL ENERGY WORKS THROUGH HUMANITY FOR THE BENEFIT OF HUMANITY. SO, LET'S SEEK TO KNOW THE POWER IN THE ENERGY OF CREATION AND THEN LET'S BEGIN TO CREATE. LET'S CREATE FOR THE BENEFIT OF OUR CHILDREN AND THEIR CHILDREN AND THEIR CHILDREN AND THEIR CHILDREN AND THEIR CHILDREN AND THEIR CHILDREN AND THEIR CHILDREN AND THEIR CHILDREN AND THEIR CHILDREN.

MY VISION FROM PRISON IS A COMPILATION OF THOUGHTS FROM VINCENT GAMBOA-HIGINIO GROWING INTO ELIMU ONE YAHSON. THE MOTIVE FOR WRITING THE BOOK IS THE HOPE THAT THE READER WILL UNDERSTAND THAT OUR BELOVED CREATOR CREATED US TO CREATIVELY CREATE OUR OWN CREATION.

WE DO OURSELVES AND OUR CREATOR A GREAT INJUSTICE WHEN WE FAIL TO CREATIVELY CREATE A CREATION THAT WILL BE HARMONIOUS TO THE SPIRITUAL, MENTAL, EMOTIONAL AND PHYSICAL PROGRESS OF OURSELVES AND OUR POSTERITY.

IT IS MY PRAYER THAT "MY VISION FROM PRISON" WILL CONVEY THE MESSAGE THAT IF OUR CHILDREN FAIL, WE FAIL.

IF OUR CHILDREN CANNOT FIND EMPLOYMENT (THAT SATISFIES THE SOUL), IT IS BECAUSE WE FAILED TO CREATE THAT BILLION DOLLAR CORPORATION, OR THAT BEAUTY SALON, OR THAT RESTAURANT, OR THAT CANDY STORE OR WHATEVER IT WAS THAT YOU CONCEIVED BUT DID NOT BELIEVE AND FAILED TO ACHIEVE.

WE FAILED OUR CHILDREN BECAUSE WE KNEW THAT THE SYSTEM WAS NOT CREATED FOR OUR BENEFIT YET FAILED TO CREATIVELY CREATE A SYSTEM THAT WOULD PROVIDE FOR THEIR WELLBEING.

WE CAN NO LONGER BLAME THE SYSTEM. WE KNOW THAT THEY WILL NOT CREATE AN ENVIRONMENT THAT WILL SERVE OUR BEST INTEREST, WE KNOW THAT THAT ENVIRONMENT MUST BE CREATED BY US IF IT IS GOING TO BE FOR US. THE QUESTION IS "DO WE HAVE THE COURAGE, COMMITMENT AND COMPASSION TO CREATIVELY CREATE A SYSTEM THAT WILL AID AND ASSIST OUR CHILDREN IN THEIR PROCESS, PROGRESS AND PURPOSE?

IF YOU'RE NOT WILLING TO BE COURAGEOUS, THEN YOU NEED TO WATCH OUT BECAUSE YOU'RE IN THE WAY AND WE ARE COMING.

LET'S CREATIVELY CREATE CREATION WITH GUIDANCE FROM THE CREATOR AND PLAY A POSITIVE AND PRODUCTIVE PART IN THE PROCESS OF PROGRESS TOWARDS PROSPERITY FOR OUR POSTERITY.

SOMEONE ELSE

WE LOOK TO SOMEONE ELSE TO FIGHT OUR FIGHT, ONLY LOOKING TO CELEBRATE THE VICTORY AND THAT AIN'T RIGHT.

WHEN YOU LOOK BACK AT YOUR HISTORY AND TRY TO FIND THE GOOD, WILL IT BE THAT YOU WAS A DOWN ASS HOMIE REPPING THE HOOD?

YOU ARE FIGHTING THE WRONG FIGHT AND YOUR CHILDREN WILL SOMEDAY SEE, THAT YOU WERE REALLY A TRICK AND A MENACE TO SOCIETY.

THINK ABOUT WHAT YOUR DOING, THEN STAND UP AND BE A MAN, THE GANGBANGING, AND DOPE SLANGING IS SOMEONE ELSE'S PLAN.

THINK ABOUT YOUR CHILDREN AND WHAT THEIR FUTURE IS GOING TO BE, LOOK AT WHERE YOU'RE AT AND REFLECT ON BEING FREE

THE SOLUTION

THE SOLUTION TO THE PROBLEM IS FOUND WITHIN THE PROBLEM. THE PROBLEM IS WE KNOW THE SOLUTION. EACH ONE OF US KNOW WHAT TO DO, WE KNOW WHAT WE CAN DO, WE KNOW WHAT WE ARE WILLING TO DO, AND WE TALK ABOUT COURAGE, COMMITMENT AND CONSISTENCY AS ESSENTIAL ELEMENTS THAT MUST BE HARMONIZED WITHIN THIS PROCESS OF PROGRESS. THE PROBLEM IS WE KNOW THESE THINGS YET FAIL TO LIVE UP TO WHAT WE KNOW IS TRUE. THE SOLUTION WILL HAVE AN IMPACT WHEN WE COURAGEOUSLY ACCEPT THE COMMITMENT TO THE SACRIFICES THAT MUST BE CONSISTENT.

WHEN WE COMMIT OURSELVES TO THE SACRIFICES THAT'S WITHIN THE SOLUTION, WE WILL BEGIN TO EXPERIENCE THE ERADICATION OF THE PROBLEM AND THE SACRIFICES WILL SIMPLY BECOME A PART OF THE PROCESS OF PROGRESS. THE SOLUTION IS TO LIVE WHAT WE KNOW TO BE TRUE. IT IS COURAGEOUS TO LIVE YOUR PURPOSE.

ARE YOU THE EXPRESSION OF YOUR DEFINITION OF LOVE?

DO YOU LOVE OTHERS AS MUCH AS YOU EXPECT OTHERS TO LOVE YOU? COULD YOU BE LOVE AND BE LOVED?

MANY OF US GREW UP IN A HOUSEHOLD WHERE WE WERE TOLD TO LOVE BUT WAS NEVER GIVEN THE COMPLETE UNDERSTANDING OF THE EXPRESSION OF LOVE.

WHEN WE WENT TO CHURCH WE WERE TOLD THAT GOD IS LOVE BUT WE WERE NOT TAUGHT WHO GOD IS.

HOW CAN WE EXPRESS LOVE WHEN WE DON'T KNOW THE TRUE DEFINITION OF LOVE?

HOW CAN WE LOVE GOD WHEN WE DON'T KNOW GOD?

HOW CAN WE KNOW GOD WHEN WE DON'T KNOW SELF?

HOW CAN WE LOVE GOD WHEN WE DON'T LOVE SELF?

LOVE IS AN ACTION WORD WHICH IS BEST EXPRESSED THROUGH WHAT WE SAY THINK AND DO BOTH TO OURSELVES AND TO OTHERS.

LOVE IS CREATING FOR HUMANITY THE SAME ENERGY OF PEACE, PROSPERITY AND PURPOSE FROM WHICH WE SEEK TO LIVE.

LOVE IS UNDERSTANDING ONE ANOTHER'S PROCESS.

LOVE IS AIDING ONE ANOTHER'S PROGRESS.

LOVE IS LIVING IN PURPOSE ON PURPOSE.

LOVE IS AN ENERGY THAT FEEDS ON ITSELF, WHEN WE PLANT THE SEED OF LOVE THE ENERGY THAT EMANATES WILL NURTURE THE SEED AND PRODUCE PURPOSEFUL BLESSINGS.

LOVE IS AN ENERGY THAT WE CAN NEVER SHARE ENOUGH OF AND THERE IS NO WRONG TIME TO SHARE LOVE.

IT IS CRITICAL THAT WE BEGIN TO CREATE A ENVIRONMENT THAT WILL BE HARMONIOUS TO THE NURTURING AND CULTURAL DEVELOPMENT OF OUR FAMILIES IN DIVINE LOVE.

LOVE IS A VERY CRITICAL ELEMENT THAT MUST BE PROPERLY UNDERSTOOD AND PROMOTED THROUGHOUT OUR DAILY LIVES. WHEN WE UNDERSTAND LOVE WE UNDERSTAND OUR PURPOSE AND RESPONSE-ABLE-I-TY NOT ONLY TO OURSELVES BUT ALSO TO HUMANITY.

WHEN WE BUILD OUR FOUNDATION ON LOVE WE ARE BUILDING ON A PRINCIPLE THAT IS SOLID AND FIRM. THIS FOUNDATION WILL NEVER CRUMBLE BECAUSE THERE IS NO FAILURE IN LOVE.

LET'S MAKE IT OUR DUTY TODAY AND EVERYDAY TO LIVE IN LOVE AND LET LOVE LIVE IN US. JUST DON'T SAY THE WORDS "I LOVE YOU", BE THE EXPRESSION OF LOVE AND BE LOVE AND TRULY YOU WILL BE LOVED.

DRIFTING ON A MEMORY

DRIFTING ON A MEMORY WHAT DO I SEE?

I SEE A KING ON A THRONE, I SEE A QUEEN SITTING ALONE.

I SEE WISE YOUNG KINGS RULING THE LAND, I SEE MISGUIDED WARRIORS WITH GUN IN HAND.

I SEE BEAUTIFUL QUEENS LIVING IN JOY, I SEE A MIDDLE AGE MAN ACTING LIKE A BOY.

WHEN YOUR MEMORY DRIFTS WHAT DO YOU SEE?

WHEN YOU DRIFT TO THE FUTURE WHAT WILL IT BE?

TO BECOME A BETTER YOU IS NEVER TO LATE, JUST HAVE FAITH IN SELF AND BEGIN TO CREATE.

KNOWLEDGE, UNDERSTANDING AND WISDOM WILL GIVE YOU POWER, THESE ARE THREE ESSENTIALS WE NEED THIS HOUR.

OUR BELOVED CREATOR CREATIVELY CREATED US TO CREATE, SITTING ON A THRONE IS OUR FATE.

GET KNOWLEDGE, LEARN UNDERSTANDING AND LOVE WISDOM, AND LET'S MOVE OUR QUEENS TO HER QUEENDOM.

LET'S PROTECT OUR QUEENS FROM THE DANGER WE SEE, LET'S CREATE A BETTER FUTURE SO OUR POSTERITY WILL BE FREE..

I'M IN PRISON AND MY WIFE/GIRLFRIEND AINT FUCKING

YEAH, YOU RIGHT. YOU KNOW YOUR WIFE/GIRLFRIEND AND SHE AINT GONNA DISRESPECT YOU, BUT WHEN YOU FINISH THAT SENTENCE THE LAST WORDS WILL BE AND LET ME FIND OUT ABOUT IT. IF YOU WERE REALLY BEING HONEST WITH YOURSELF YOU WOULD SAY, "I KNOW BABY GIRL IS GONNA MISS ME BEATING THAT THANG UP DOGGIE STYLE, AND SHE DEFINITELY GONNA MISS THEM TRIPLE ORGASMS WHEN I USE TO LICK THAT COOCHIE LIKE STRAWBERRY ICE CREAM. BUT THAT'S ONLY HALF THE STORY.

WHEN YOU REALLY GO DEEP IN THOUGHT YOU WILL REALIZE THAT SEX WILL ONLY BE A SMALL PART OF THE RELATIONSHIP THAT SHE'S GONNA MISS. SHE'S GONNA MISS YOUR LAUGHTER, YOUR COMPANIONSHIP, YOUR WORDS OF ENCOURAGEMENT, YOUR WISDOM, YOUR GUIDANCE AND YOUR UNIQUE WAY OF MAKING HER FEEL SPECIAL. SHE'S MISSING THAT SENSE OF SECURITY OF KNOWING THAT YOU ARE THERE WITH HER AND FOR HER AND THAT YOU HAVE HER BACK NO MATTER WHAT.

NOW SHE COMES TO A EMPTY HOUSE, SHE EATS ALONE, SHE SHOWERS ALONE, GO TO BED ALONE AND WAKES UP IN YA'LL BIG ASS KING SIZE BED ALL ALONE.

SHE DOESN'T REALLY HAVE ANYONE TO TALK TO BECAUSE YOU ARE ONE OF A KIND, YOU LISTENED TO HER AND DID YOUR BEST TO UNDERSTAND HER. YOU ARE A GREAT MAN AND SHE MISSES YOU SO MUCH.

SHE MISSES YOU SO MUCH SHE SEES A LITTLE BIT OF YOU IN EVERY MAN SHE SEES. HER CO-WORKER LAUGHS JUST LIKE YOU, THE GAS STATION ATTENDANT HAS YOUR EYES, THE MAILMAN WALKS LIKE YOU. IF SHE COULD FIND A LITTLE BIT OF YOU IN A MAN IT WILL BE BETTER THAN HAVING NONE OF YOU. SHE KNOWS THAT NO ONE CAN REPLACE ALL OF YOU BUT THERE IS SOME OF YOU THAT CAN BE REPLACED. AT FIRST IT'S ABOUT HAVING A COMPANION, SOMEONE TO TALK WITH SOMEONE TO LAUGH WITH, SOMEONE TO EAT WITH.

AT FIRST THE SEX IS NOT AS IMPORTANT TO HER AS IT IS TO HIM. BUT WHEN HE LEAVES SHE'S IN BED ALL ALONE REMEMBERING HOW YOU USED TO BLOW HER BACK OUT, AFTER AWHILE HER FINGERS AND THE SEX TOYS CAN'T GET HER OFF NO MORE. YOU KNOW THE REST.

I WRITE THIS FOR THE GUYS IN THE STREETS THROWING ROCKS AT THE PENITENTIARY AND FOR THOSE JUST COMING INTO THE SYSTEM. TO THE FELLOWS IN THE STREETS, IF YOU GOT A GOOD WOMAN AND YOU DON'T WANT TO LOSE HER OR SHARE HER WITH SOMEONE ELSE, CHECK YOURSELF AND RENAME YOUR GAME.

TO THOSE OF YOU JUST GETTING LOCKED UP, DO YOUR BEST TO UNDERSTAND WHAT SHE IS ABOUT TO EXPERIENCE. YOU WERE A VERY SPECIAL PART OF HER LIFE AND NOW YOU'RE MISSING. WE ALL HAVE NEEDS, WANTS AND DESIRES AND WE WILL FIND WAYS TO HAVE THEM FULFILLED. ACCEPTING THIS AS TRUTH YOU MUST KNOW THAT YOU ARE NOW IN A POSITION TO FULFILL HER EMOTIONALLY, MENTALLY AND SPIRITUALLY. BUT IN ORDER TO DO THIS YOU MUST FIRST ELEVATE YOUR LEVEL OF INTELLIGENCE IN THESE AREAS. USE YOUR TIME TO GET TO KNOW YOURSELF AND IN DOING SO YOU WILL BE BETTER EQUIPT IN KNOWING AND UNDERSTANDING YOUR WOMAN.

I KNOW IT HURTS TO ACCEPT AS TRUTH THAT THE WOMAN YOU LOVE IS LAYING IN YALL KING SIZE BED ASS HOLE NAKED GETTING WORKED OVER BY ANOTHER MAN, HOWEVER, THE FACT REMAINS THAT SHE MISSES YOU JUST AS MUCH AS YOU MISS HER AND SHE WILL NEED THE UNDERSTANDING, GUIDANCE, SUPPORT AND UNCONDITIONAL LOVE THAT YOU WILL EXPECT FROM HER.

BE HONEST WITH YOURSELF WHEN YOU ANSWER THIS QUESTION 'HOW WOULD YOU ACT IF YOUR WOMAN WAS IN JAIL"?

PROGRESS AND PAIN A-GAIN

I FELL DOWN AND IT HURT REAL BAD, I GOT UP AND I FELT SO GLAD.

I GOT BEAT UP IN A FIGHT, I KICKED ASS ON THE VERY NEXT NIGHT.

MY QUEEN LOVED ME, THEN SHE LOVED ME NOT, NOW WE ARE ONE AND WE LOVE A LOT.

PROGRESS IN PROCESS ON PURPOSE IS A MUST, AND PAIN A-GAIN IS A FRIEND YOU CAN TRUST.

LIFE EXPERIENCES ARE TO BE USED AS TOOLS, KNOWLEDGE, UNDERSTANDING AND WISDOM ARE IN BOOKS AND IN SCHOOLS.

YOU DON'T KNOW IT ALL, THIS YOU MUST KNOW, UNDERSTANDING PAIN A-GAIN WILL SURELY HELP YOU GROW.

PAIN WILL TEACH US WHAT WE DID WRONG ON A SPIRITUAL PLANE AND WE WILL PROGRESS WITH THIS WISDOM AND PROCESS A GAIN FROM PAIN.

BLACK FOLKS FINALLY MADE IT TO THE TOP

WHEN IT COMES TO DEGRADATION, INCARCERATION AND MISEDUCATION WE ARE AT THE TOP, WHEN IT COMES TO RELAXATION, LIBERATION AND EMANCIPATION OUR STATUS TENDS TO DROP.

WHEN IT COMES TO EXPLOITATION, SUFFERATION AND DEFAMATION OUR NUMBERS TEND TO RISE, WHEN IT COMES TO ORGANIZATION, MOBILIZATION AND PARTICIPATION OUR UNITY SLOWLY DIES.

AT THE TOP OF EVERY NEGATIVE STAT WE SEE BLACK FOLK, WE CLAIM TO BE KINGS AND QUEENS BUT WERE LOOKED AT AS A JOKE.

THEY LAUGH AT US, MAKE FUN OF US AND CALL US FOUL NAMES, WE CALL OURSELVES BOSS PLAYERS BUT WERE JUST PAWNS IN THEIR GAMES.

YEAH, WE MADE IT TO THE TOP BLACK FOLKS AND THINGS SEEMS TO BE LEGIT, THE TOP OF EVERY NEGATIVE STAT AND REALLY THAT AIN'T SHIT.

LET'S GET OFF THEIR MOUNTAIN AND BUILD OUR OWN.

RENAME THE GAME

THE STREET GAME BROUGHT US FAME, IT EVEN GAVE A LAME A NAME. WE SHOWED NO SHAME OUR URGES WE WOULDN'T TAME AS WE SEXED THE FINEST DAMES. WHAT WAS OUR AIM? THE MILLION DOLLARS NEVER CAME, NOW OUR FAMILIES ARE MAIM AND GUESS WHO'S THE BLAME?

THE THOUGHT WAS CORRECT, WE WANTED TO PROVIDE, BUT WE LOST FOCUS WHEN WE BOUGHT OUR FIFTH RIDE.

THAT ONE WAS FOR LITTLE VINCENT THAT'S HOW WE SAID IT WOULD BE, BUT HOW COULD LITTLE VINCENT DRIVE, MAN, HE WAS ONLY THREE.

WE WOULD BUY ANOTHER HOUSE AND THEN WE WOULD STOP, BUT WE STILL HAD HALF A BIRD WHEN THE HOMIE TOLD THE COP.

IT WASN'T MY HOMIE, THAT'S WHAT WE WANTED TO BELIEVE, LITTLE DID WE KNOW, US FOR LESS TIME IS WHAT HE WANTED TO ACHIEVE.

WE WERE ASKED TO SNITCH ON THREE, BUT WE STAYED STRONG, NOW WE'RE IN THE PENITENTIARY WITH A SENTENCE THIRTY YEARS LONG.

NOW WE ARE WONDERING WHAT WE COULD HAVE DONE WITH OUR LIFE, AND THE OTHER HOMIE DONE MOVED IN AND HE'S SEXING THE WIFE.

SHE STILL ACCEPTS YOUR CALLS AND SHE VISITS EVERY WEEK, BUT SHE MISSES YOUR GOOD LOVING, NOW IT'S YOUR HOMIE THAT SHE FREAKS.

LITTLE VINCENT REALLY MISSES YOU AND THE HOMIE NOW TAKES HIM TO SCHOOL, SOON THEY WILL BE MOVING INTO A NEW HOUSE, REMEMBER THE ONE WITH THE POOL?

THE HOMIE WORKED HARD STAYED FOCUSED AND GOT A JOB, HE PUT HIS THOUGHTS TOGETHER, GOT CREATIVE, BOUGHT HIS OWN BUSINESS AND NOW CALLS IT BOB.

NOW HE GOT THAT MILLION DOLLARS THAT YOU WERE TRYING TO GET, HE IS DOING SO DAMN GOOD HE'S ABOUT TO BUY A JET.

DON'T WORRY LITTLE VINCENT WILL BE ABLE TO RIDE, YOU SEE, BOB IS NOW HIS DADDY SINCE YOU'RE NOT THERE TO PROVIDE.

DON'T BLAME THE DAME, RENAME THE GAME AND RECLAIM YOUR FAME.

THOUGHTS

THOUGHT WE WERE BALLING NOW THE FEDS GOT US CRAWLING, COLLECT CALLING AND OUR STATUS HAS FALLING.

THOUGHT WE OWNED THE WORLD BECAUSE WE WORE A JHERI CURL AND COULD SEX ANY GIRL.

THOUGHT WE DIDN'T STINK, HENNESSY WAS OUR DRINK, BUT OUR MINDS DIDN'T THINK ABOUT BEING IN THE CLINK.

THOUGHT WE WAS COOL WHEN WE DIDN'T GO TO SCHOOL BECAUSE WE DIDN'T LIKE THE RULE.

THOUGHT WE WAS FLY WHEN WE TOLD A LIE THAT MADE OUR GIRL CRY NOW THE WELL IS DRY.

THOUGHTS LEADS TO ACTS THAT BECOMES FACTS THAT DOESN'T RETRACT, SO THINK WITH TACT AND CREATE AN IMPACT THAT WILL LEAVE OUR FAMILIES INTACT.

IS IT WISE?

IS IT WISE TELLING LIES, ACTING AS IF WE DON'T HEAR THE CRIES OR SEE THE TEARS FALLING FROM THE EYES OF OUR CHILDREN WHO THEY DESPISE?

IS IT WISE TO MESMERIZE AND CONCEPTUALIZE SEEKING ONLY TO BRUTALIZE AND INSTITUTIONALIZE?

IS IT WISE TO DISGUISE THE LIES THAT PARALYZE THE EYES FROM SEEING THE PRIZE?

IS IT WISE TO HARMONIZE AND INTERNALIZE ONLY TO DEMONIZE THOSE WHO PATRONIZE?

IT IS WISE TO ORGANIZE, STABILIZE, HARMONIZE AND MOBILIZE DETERMINED TO OSTRACIZE THOSE TRYING TO LEGALIZE THE DEMISE OF THE WISE.

WATCH OUT

WATCH OUT FOR ME, WATCH OUT FOR YOU, WATCH OUT FOR THE LIES THEY SAY ARE TRUE.

WATCH OUT FOR THE THIEF THAT ROBS BY DAY, WATCH OUT FOR THE MANY TRAPS THAT WILL COME YOUR WAY.

WATCH OUT FOR THE WHITE WHO LOOKS BLACK, WATCH OUT FOR THE BLACK THAT'S UNDER ATTACK.

WATCH OUT FOR THE CHILD THAT NEVER SMILES, WATCH OUT FOR THE WISDOM THAT COMES FROM TRIALS.

WATCH OUT FOR THE EVIL THAT SURROUNDS US AT BIRTH, WATCH OUT FOR THE LOVE THAT SURROUNDS THE EARTH.

WATCH OUT FOR THE KILLA HE MIGHT LOOK LIKE ME, WATCH OUT FOR THE SAVIOR HE MIGHT BE A SHE.

THE SPIRIT OF GOD IS THE BEST

THE SPIRIT OF GOD IS THE BEST, SPIRITUAL CONSCIOUSNESS IS THE TEST.

THE SPIRIT OF GOD IS THE BEST, SPIRITUAL KINGDOM IS THE BLESS.

THE SPIRIT OF GOD IS THE BEST, SPIRITUAL BALANCE CLEARS THE MESS.

THE SPIRIT OF GOD IS THE BEST, SPIRITUAL UNDERSTANDING WILL GIVE YOU REST.

THE SPIRIT OF GOD IS THE BEST, SPIRITUAL WISDOM IS ONENESS.

THE SPIRIT OF GOD IS THE BEST, DON'T EVER SETTLE FOR ANYTHING LESS.

WHATABOUTU

THEY CALL US CRIMINALS, YET THEY ROB US OF OUR HUMANITY. WHEN THEY INTENTIONALLY DO WRONG, THEY CALL IT A MISTAKE, BUT WHEN WE MAKE A MISTAKE, THEY PUNISH US AS IF THOUGH IT WAS INTENTIONAL.

HOW CAN YOU TEACH ANYONE ANYTHING OF VALUE WHEN YOUR HEART AND MIND IS CLOSED TO ANY FORM OF SENSIBLE REASONING?

LOOK AT ME, AND THEN LOOK AT YOU, AM I A HUMAN TOO?

IF YOU CAN SEE MY HUMANITY, THEN WHY DO YOU TREAT ME LESS THAN?

IF YOU THINK THIS HURTS ME, YOU ARE CORRECT, BUT CAN YOU IMAGINE WHAT IT'S DOING TO YOU? THE LEAST YOU DO UNTO HUMANITY, THE SAME YOU DO UNTO GOD.

DON'T ALLOW MAN-MADE LAWS TO SUPERSEDE GOD'S LAW. PROTECT YOUR SPIRIT AND HOLD HUMANITY HIGH. LIVE WISELY AND DO NOT ALLOW MAN-MADE LAWS TO GOVERN YOUR THOUGHTS. GOD IS THE LAW GIVER AND IF MAN=MADE LAWS DIFFER IN THE SLIGHTEST DEGREE FROM THE LAWS GIVEN TO US BY GOD, WE ARE TO DETECT THE EVIL IN THEM AND CAREFULLY AND WISELY DISREGARD THEM.

FROM ONE HUMAN TO ANOTHER, PLEASE RESPECT MY HUMANITY AND I WILL RESPECT YOURS.

SOME GO TO PRISON

SOME GO TO PRISON BY FORCE, SOME GO TO PRISON BY CHOICE.

SOME GO TO PRISON AND PRAY, SOME GO TO PRISON FOR PAY.

SOME GO TO PRISON EVERY HOUR, SOME GO TO PRISON FOR POWER.

SOME GO TO PRISON AND LOOSE, SOME GO TO PRISON FOR CLUES.

SOME GO TO PRISON AND DIE, SOME GO TO PRISON AND LIE.

SOME GO TO PRISON AND PLEAD, SOME GO TO PRISON IN NEED.

SOME GO TO PRISON AND GROW, SOME ARE IN PRISON AND DON'T EVEN KNOW.

CREATE CREATION

SOCIETY IS CREATED FROM THE VISION OF THOSE WHO UNDERSTAND THROUGH KNOWLEDGE AND THE APPLICATION OF WISDOM, THE WONDERFUL BLESSING THAT OUR BELOVED CREATOR CREATED US TO CREATIVELY CREATE A CREATION BASED ON THE PRINCIPLES OF LOVE, PEACE, JOY, RIGHTEOUSNESS, PROSPERITY, FREE-DOME, AND JUSTICE. LET'S MAKE SURE THAT OUR VISION CREATES A SOCIETY IN WHICH OUR CHILDREN CAN ENJOY HEAVEN RIGHT HERE ON EARTH. OUR BELOVED CREATOR WILL GUIDE US WITH CREATIVITY AND TEACH US HOW TO CREATE A BEAUTIFUL SOCIETY FOR OUR POSTERITY. BE WISE AND ALLOW OUR BELOVED CREATOR TO CREATIVELY CREATE THROUGH YOU.

BIG PROBLEM

SINGLE FAMILY HOMES ARE A BIG PROBLEM. CHILDREN HAVING CHILDREN HAS CREATED AN ENVIRONMENT WHEREIN THE BLIND IS LEADING THE BLIND.

HOW CAN WE EXPECT OUR CHILDREN TO TEACH THEIR CHILDREN ANYTHING OF VALUE WHEN WE HAVE TAUGHT THEM HALF TRUTHS AND SOMETIMES JUST STRAIGHT UP LIED?

WE HAVE BOWED DOWN TO A SYSTEM OF MORAL CONDUCT AND VALUES THAT IS DESTROYING OUR FAMILIES, IN ORDER TO SOLVE THIS PROBLEM, WE MUST FIRST RE-EDUCATE OURSELVES IN GOD AND THEN RE-EDUCATE THE GOD IN US. WE ARE SERVING THE WRONG GOD.

RESPONSE-ABILITY

THE MISEDUCATION OF OUR PEOPLE IS PROFOUND, AND IT IS THE RESPONSE-ABILITY OF THOSE OF US WHO HAS RE-EDUCATED OURSELVES TO NOT ONLY SHARE OUR WISDOM WITH EACH OTHER, BUT TO ALSO MAKE SURE THAT OUR CHILDREN AND THEIR CHILDREN'S CHILDREN'S RECEIVE THE PROPER EDUCATION NOT JUST IN THE SCHOOLS, BUT MORE IMPORTANT AT HOME.

WE MUST BEGIN TO UNDERSTAND THE ENERGY OF CREATION AND BECOME ONE WITH THIS CREATIVE FORCE.

IT IS CRITICAL THAT WE BECOME CREATORS AND CREATE THE ENVIRONMENT THAT WILL BEST SERVE THE PHYSICAL, SPIRITUAL AND MENTAL NEEDS OF OUR PEOPLE.

WE CANNOT CONTINUE TO ALLOW THIS SYSTEM TO MIS-EDUCATE OUR CHILDREN AND CREATE FOR US AND THEM A VALUE SYSTEM VOID OF MORALS AND INTEGRITY. IT IS IMPERATIVE THAT WE BEGIN TO UNDERSTAND THE PRINCIPLES OF THE ONENESS OF GOD AND BECOME CREATORS OF THE ENVIRONMENT WHEREIN WE CAN TEACH THE VALUE OF LOVE, TRUTH, FREE-DOME, JUSTICE AND RIGHTEOUSNESS. I BELIEVE IN ME. DO YOU BELIEVE IN YOU?

THE GRASS AND ROOTS

THE TEACHINGS OF HISTORY REMINDS US OF OUR BROTHERS AND SISTER'S THE MAROONS. OUR BROTHERS AND SISTERS FOUGHT VICTORIOUSLY FROM THE MORAL CENTER OF THEIR SOULS. THE MAROONS UNDERSTOOD THAT IF THEY COULD CREATE THE ENVIRONMENT THAT WOULD PROTECT THE MORAL VALUES AND INTEGRITY OF THEIR CULTURE THEN THEY WOULD BE ABLE TO PRESERVE THE SPIRITUAL, MENTAL, EMOTIONAL AND PHYSICAL WELL BEING OF THEIR CHILDREN AND THEIR CHILDREN'S CHILDRENS'. THE MAROONS FOUGHT IN THE JUNGLE AMONG THE GRASS AND ROOTS AND TODAY OUR BROTHER'S AND SISTERS ARE STILL FIGHTING FROM THE MORAL CENTER OF THEIR SOULS AMONG THE GRASSROOTS. LET'S JOIN THE FIGHT FOR OUR RIGHTS WITH THE LIGHT SHINING BRIGHT, FOR THIS IS OUR BIRTHRIGHT.

ACT NOW

WE HAVE A MAJOR PROBLEM IN OUR COMMUNITIES, AND WE MUST ACT NOW. OUR TALK AND DO NOTHING BEHAVIOR HAS ALLOWED A VERY WICKED, EVIL AND DESTRUCTIVE ENERGY TO CREATE FOR US AN ENVIRONMENT THAT CONTINUES TO LOSE ITS VALUES AND MORAL INTEGRITY. THIS EVIL AND DESTRUCTIVE ENERGY HAS CREATED A GENERATION OF BROKEN HOMES, WHICH CREATES BROKEN INDIVIDUALS, WHICH LEADS TO ANOTHER GENERATION OF BROKEN CHILDREN. WE ARE LIVING BELOW THE POVERTY RATE OUR CHILDREN ARE RECEIVING AN INFERIOR EDUCATION AND WE ARE STILL JUST TALKING. OUR CULTURE CONTINUES TO BE SYSTEMATICALLY ERADICATED WHILE AT THE SAME TIME WE ARE BEING MANIPULATED INTO A LIFESTYLE LACKING IN STRENGTH, HONOR AND NOBILITY. IF WE ARE AS REAL AND TRUE TO THE STRUGGLE AS WE CLAIM TO BE, WE WILL MAKE SURE THAT WE ARE LEADING THE WAY. UNTIL WE STEP UP AND MAKE IT OUR RESPONSE-ABILITY TO CREATE A BRIGHTER AND BETTER TOMORROW FOR OUR CHILDREN, WE MUST PREPARE THEM FOR PRISON, AIDS, POVERTY AND SELF-DESTRUCTION. IF WE DON'T CREATE OUR OWN GAME WITH OUR OWN RULES, WE WILL CONTINUE TO LOOSE AND SO WILL OUR CHILDREN.

IS HE? IS SHE?

IS SHE YOUR WOMAN? IS HE YOUR MAN? IS SHE YOUR FRIEND? IS HE YOUR FAN?

DOES SHE REALLY LOVE YOU? DOES HE REALLY CARE? DOES SHE LISTEN TO YOUR CONCERNS? DOES HE TREAT YOU FAIR?

WOULD YOU MARRY HIM TOMORROW? WOULD YOU LOVE HIM FOR LIFE? COULD HE BE THAT SPECIAL SOMEONE? COULD YOU BE THAT LOVING WIFE?

WHEN YOU HOLD HIM IN YOUR ARMS DOES IT STILL FEEL LIKE EXTASY? WHEN YOU HOLD HER IN YOUR ARMS DO YOU STILL FEEL FREE?

IF YOU ANSWERED YES TO THESE QUESTIONS THEN YOU KNOW THE LOVE IS TRUE, YOU HAVE FOUND YOUR SOULMATE AND HAVE BECOME ONE, YOU'RE NO LONGER TWO.

MY CHILD, YOUR CHILD, OUR CHILD.

MY CHILD YOUR CHILD OUR CHILD WHAT WILL WE TEACH HIM? MY CHILD YOUR CHILD OUR CHILD HOW WILL WE REACH HIM?

YOUR CHILD OUR CHILD MY CHILD HOW WILL WE RAISE HER? YOUR CHILD OUR CHILD MY CHILD HOW WILL WE PRAISE HER?

OUR CHILD MY CHILD YOUR CHILD THEY ARE OUR RESPONSIBILITY. OUR CHILD MY CHILD YOUR CHILD LET'S LOVE THEM SINCERELY.

CRACK THE MACK?

LET'S LOOK AT CRACK THE MACK WHO CAME IN A SACK, BROUGHT US A STACK, SO WE COULD BUY OFF THE RACK, OWN OUR OWN SHACK AND RUN THE PACK.

CRACK WAS THE MACK THAT PUT OUR SISTERS ON THEIR BACK AND OUR BROTHERS ON THE RACK. LITTLE DID WE KNOW WE WAS UNDER ATTACK FROM A PACK OF WACK HACKS WITH SHEETS ON THEIR BACKS WHO DIDN'T LIKE BLACK.

THE SHACK CAME UNDER ATTACK, THEY FOUND THE CRACK, THEY STOLE THE SACK, TOOK THE CLOTHES OFF THE RACK, NOW WE'RE ON OUR BACK AND OUR PACK IS WACK.

MACK THE BLACK, CRACK IS WACK, ATTACK BACK, UNRACK THE PACK.

DO YOU

DO YOU BREED TO FEED THE SEED THAT WILL LEAD NOT PLEAD OR CONCEDE TO THE MISDEED OF THE GREED?

DO YOU SOW WHAT WILL GROW TO SHOW THE LOW THINGS TO KNOW WHAT WILL OPEN THE DOE FOR THE POE.

DO YOU WALK THE TALK OR STALK THE CHALK THAT REMOVES THE DARK LEFT BY THE SHARK WITH THE VICIOUS BARK WHO SINGS LIKE A LARK?

DO YOU PREACH TO REACH AND TEACH WITH SPEECH WHAT WILL BESEECH EACH AND SCREECH THE LEECH?

BETTER CREATORS

WHEN WE TAKE A SERIOUS LOOK AT THE WORLD TODAY WE WILL SEE AN ALARMING INCREASE OF DEGRADATION AND THE MORAL INTEGRITY OF THE MAJORITY HAS CONSISTENTLY TAKEN A SPIRAL JOURNEY INTO THE ABYSS. IF WE REALLY AND TRULY LOVE OURSELVES AND IF WE REALLY AND TRULY HAVE ANY CONCERN FOR THE WELL=BEING OF OUR POSTERITY WE MUST STEP UP AND BECOME BETTER CREATOR'S. BE MINDFUL THAT WHAT WE CREATE OR ALLOW TO BE CREATED IN THIS WORLD TODAY WILL BE LEFT FOR OUR CHILDREN TO DEAL WITH TOMORROW.

DIAMOND OR ROCK

EVEN WHEN WE HIT A ROCK WE MUST CAREFULLY ANALYZE THE ROCKS MAKE UP. ALL TOO OFTEN WE TEND TO MISTAKE THE ROCK FOR SOMETHING JUST PLAIN AND ORDINARY. HOWEVER, AFTER CAREFUL AND CRITICAL ANALYSIS WE WILL REALIZE THAT THE ROCK WE HIT WAY DOWN AT THE BOTTOM WAS ACTUALLY A DIAMOND.

TRICKED YA

RACIAL DISCRIMINATION IS OFTEN VERY DIFFICULT TO PROVE. WE OFTEN CHOOSE TO RUNAWAY FROM THESE ISSUES AS IF THOUGH THEY WILL SIMPLY JUST GO AWAY. HOWEVER, THE FACTS OF LIFE WILL DOUBTLESSLY PROVE THAT RACISM DOES EXIST IN TODAY'S WORLD AND ITS PRACTICE HAS BECOME VERY VERY SOPHISTICATED. DON'T GET IT TWISTED THEY STILL DON'T LIKE YOUR BLACK ASS.

IF THEY RUIN YOU, YOU WILL RUIN US!

PRESIDENT OBAMA, PLEASE STAND STRONG, FOLLOWING YOUR MORAL CONSCIENCE COULD NEVER BE WRONG.

YOU SEE THEIR PLANS AND KNOW IT AIN'T RIGHT, YOU HAVE BEEN CHOSEN TO LEAD THIS FIGHT.

FEAR OF DEATH SHOULD NEVER BE THE REASON, TO BETRAY YOUR MORAL CONSCIENCE IS AN ACT OF TREASON.

CAP AND TRADE BANK BAILOUTS AND HEALTHCARE, WHO GAVE THE ADVICE THAT LED YOU THERE?

THEY PAT YOU ON THE BACK AND SMILE IN YOUR FACE, THEY EVEN PRETEND THEY DON'T NOTICE YOUR RACE.

ONE PERCENT OF BLACK BLOOD MAKES YOU A KEMETIAN, FAITH IN GOD AND SELF MAKES YOU A FREE MAN.

THEY ARE PEOPLE IN YOUR OWN PARTY WHO WANTS YOU TO FAIL, IT'S THE SELF-ESTEEM, GOALS AND FAITH OF OUR FUTURE GENERATION THEY SEEK TO DERAIL.

WHAT WILL BE YOUR LEGACY SHOULD BE YOUR CONCERN, WILL IT BE A PRESIDENCY FROM WHICH OUR CHILDREN COULD LEARN?

YOU HAVE A LOVELY WIFE AND TWO BEAUTIFUL DAUGHTERS, NAT, MARCUS, MALCOLM, MARTIN, OUR HONORABLE FOREFATHERS.

TO DIE FOR A BETTER FUTURE IS AN HONORABLE DEED, TO LIVE FOR OUR FUTURE GENERATION MUST BE OUR CREED.

OUR CHILDREN IS WATCHING EVERYTHING YOU DO, SOME OF THEM WANT TO GROW UP AND BECOME PRESIDENT TWO.

WILL YOU LEAD THEM WITH COURAGE, COMMITMENT, AND FAITH, OR WILL YOU CONTINUE THE DECEPTION OF POLITICS THAT BREED HATE?

PRESIDENT BARACK HUSEIN OBAMA THE DECISION IS YOURS, PLEASE LEARN FROM THE COURAGE OF OUR ANCESTORS AND CONTINUE TO BREAK DOWN THEM DOORS.

STOP THE RUST WIPE THE DUST

WE TALK ABOUT THE WHITE MAN AND HIS MANY ATROCITIES, THEN WE ASK HIM FOR HIS HELP AND EXPECT THIS TO BE FREE.

THE MAN AIN'T DUMB HE CREATED THE SITUATION, WAR, POVERTY, DRUG ADDICTION AND HIV IS JUST A REVELATION.

HE KNEW WHAT WAS BEING CREATED AND HE JUST LET IT BE, HE SAID "WHAT THE FUCK" AS LONG AS IT DON'T COME BACK ON ME.

MANY OF US KNOW THIS YET STILL EXPECT HIM TO BE CONCERNED, WE WOULD HAVE THOUGHT THAT SLAVERY, JIM CROW, MASS INCARCERATION AND POLICE BRUTALITY WOULD BE LESSONS FROM WHICH WE WOULD LEARN.

WHAT'S THE FUSS? THERE IS NO NEED TO CUSS. UNITY IS A MUST. LET'S EARN EACH OTHER'S TRUST AND FILL UP THE BUS IN ORDER TO STOP THE RUST AND WIPE THE DUST AND THE PUSS FROM OUR CRUST.

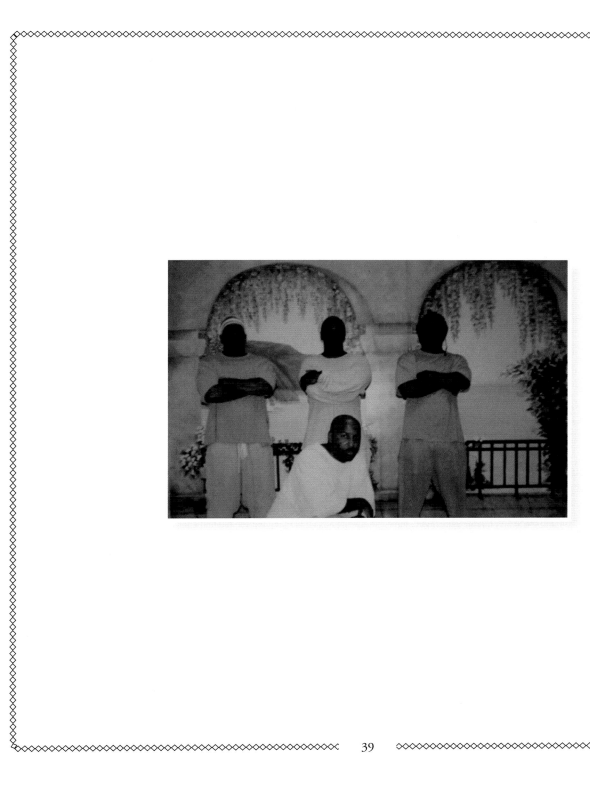

GROWING UP

WHAT IT THIS PROCESS OF GROWING? WHAT IS THIS JOURNEY?

WE LIVE TO LEARN THEN WE LEARN TO LIVE. WE LEARN TO LOVE THEN WE LOVE TO LOVE. WE LIVE TO UNDERSTAND THE ENERGY THAT CREATED CREATION AND THEN WE LEARN TO BECOME ONE WITH THIS AWESOME ENERGY.

PURPOSE IS POWER, AND IT IS A BLESSING TO KNOW AND LOVE YOUR PURPOSE. ITS FOUNDATION IS FIRMLY PLANTED WITHIN US AND IT IS US.

UNDERSTANDING OUR PURPOSE IS KNOWING THAT WE ARE HERE FOR A DIVINE MISSION. KNOWING OUR PURPOSE IS LIVING IN ONENESS WITH THE DIVINE MIND OF THE CREATOR AND CREATIVELY CREATING OUR OWN CREATION.

GROW UP AND LIVE YOUR PURPOSE. GROW UP AND LOVE YOUR PURPOSE. GROW UP AND LOVE TRUTH, GROW UP AND LIVE TRUTH.

UNDERSTAND CREATION AND CREATE LOVE. GROW UP AND LEARN SELF AND THEN LOVE SELF. LIVE IN LOVE AND LET LOVE LIVE IN YOU.

GROWING UP IS THE PROCESS OF UNDERSTANDING THE ENERGY WITHIN THE ONENESS OF CREATION AND THEN BECOMING ONE WITH THIS DIVINE ENERGY. GROWING UP IS ENERGY IN PROCESS WITH PURPOSE.

GROWING UP IS A SPIRITUAL PROCESS AND IT IS OUR RESPONSE-ABILITY TO CREATION TO LIVE IN ONENESS WITH THE DIVINE MIND OF OUR CREATOR AND CREATIVELY CREATE OUR OWN CREATION ON PURPOSE TOWARDS PROSPERITY FOR OUR POSTERITY.

THE QUEST

THE QUEST TO OPPRESS THE BLESS REFUSING TO CONFESS THEIR PLAN TO COMPRESS THE REST WITH LESS THAN THE BEST IS A MESS IN THE WEST.

THE QUEST TO BE THE BEST IS A CONSTANT TEST IN THE WEST AND WE CANNOT REST UNLESS WE CONTEST THE MESS THAT CAUSES US TO DIGRESS, REPRESS AND ACHIEVE LESS THAN THE REST.

THE QUEST TO REST IS ACHIEVED BY THE BEST WHO PASSED THE TEST REFUSING TO DIGRESS, REPRESS OR OPPRESS THE COURAGE IN THE CHEST, AND WE WILL BLESS THE REST AND WIN THE CONTEST REGARDLESS OF THE MESS BECAUSE WE HAVE THE ANSWERS TO THE TEST.

REFORM, CONFORM & DEFORM

THEY REFORM OUR MINDS, WE CONFORM OUR ACTIONS, AND DEFORM BECOMES OUR CULTURE.

THEY TAUGHT US HOW TO THINK NOW WE DO WHAT THEY DO. KILLING HAS BECOME ANOTHER FORM OF RECREATION AND OUR WOMAN ARE OBJECTS ONLY FOR SEXUAL GRATIFICATION, IF A CHILD IS PRODUCED, SO WHAT.

OUR WOMEN USE TO BE QUEENS OUR FAMILY USE TO BE A TEAM AND OUR CHILDREN USE TO DREAM.

OUR MINDS HAVE BEEN REFORMED AS OUR ACTIONS CONTINUE TO CONFORM TO A CULTURE THAT IS DEFORM.

OUR DEED

WHAT IS OUR CREED, WHAT WILL BE OUR DEED ARE WE WILLING TO BLEED?

WILL WE PROCEED TO TEACH THOSE IN NEED HOW TO BE FREED OR WILL WE RECEDE AND CONCEDE TO THE MISDEED OF THE GREED?

WHAT WILL BE OUR DEED, ARE WE WILLING TO BLEED, WHAT IS OUR CREED?

INDEED WE MUST READ IN ORDER TO FEED THE SEED WE BREED.

ARE WE WILLING TO BLEED, WHAT IS OUR CREED, WHAT WILL BE OUR DEED?

LET IT BE AGREED THAT WE WILL FEED THE SEED WE BREED. TAKE HEED WHEN WE READ. INTERCEDE WITH SPEED AND IMPEDE THE MISDEED OF THE GREED, BECAUSE IT IS OUR CHILDREN WHO ARE IN NEED.

THIS IS OUR CREED, THIS IS OUR DEED AND HELL YEAH WE WILL BLEED FOR OUR SEED WHENEVER THEY NEED.

NEW WORLD ORDER

POLI-TRICK-IONS OPERATE IN SECRECY BECAUSE SECRECY IS THE LAWS AND CODES FROM WHICH THEY LIVE BY, THEIR GOAL IS WORLD DOMINATION AND THEY ARE CONSTANTLY AND CONSISTENTLY IMPLEMENTING THEIR AGENDA.

THESE PEOPLE HAVE STUDIED THE WISDOM OF OUR ANCIENT ANCESTORS AND NOW THEY UNDERSTAND WHAT OUR ANCESTORS UNDERSTOOD.

OUR ANCESTORS TAUGHT US THE ONENESS OF GOD AND THE IMPORTANCE OF HARMONIOUSLY BALANCING OUR ENERGY WITH THE DIVINE ENERGY WITHIN CREATION. WHILE THEY ARE STUDYING THE WISDOM FROM THE ANCIENT MYSTERY SYSTEM (WHICH WAS CREATED BY OUR ANCIENT ANCESTORS) AND LEARNING HOW TO BECOME CREATORS AND WE ARE BEING MANIPULATED INTO WORSHIPPING A GOD CREATED FOR US BY THEM.

THE AGENDA OF OUR SO-CALLED POLITICAL LEADERS IS TO CONTROL THE MINDS, SPIRITS AND THE PHYSICAL ACTIVITIES OF THE ENTIRE WORLD. THESE PEOPLE ARE OPERATING IN ACCORDANCE WITH A VOW OF SECRECY TAKEN MANY YEARS BEFORE OBTAINING THEIR PRESENT POLITICAL POSITION. THESE POLITICIANS ARE VERY DANGEROUS AND THEIR AGENDA IS A NEW WORLD ORDER, THE ORDER WILL BE LAID DOWN BY THEM BUT IT WON'T BE APPLICABLE TO THEM. WHENEVER THE OPPORTUNITY PRESENTS ITSELF, DO YOURSELF A FAVOR AND ASK THEM WHO IS THEIR REAL MASTER. I CAN PROMISE YOU THAT GOD WILL NOT BE THE RESPONSE.

POLI-TRICKS

OUR ELECTED OFFICIALS WAS PUT IN OFFICE TO REPRESENT THE NEEDS AND DESIRES OF OUR COMMUNITIES. DURING THEIR CAMPAIGN THEY MADE PROMISES TO US AND ASKED US TO TRUST THEM, HAVE FAITH IN THEM, AND PERSEVERE WITH THEM, SO WE VOTED FOR THEM.

LITTLE DID WE REALIZE THAT DURING THIS SAME CAMPAIGN BUT ON THE OTHER SIDE OF THE TRAIL, THESE SAME POLITICIANS WERE MAKING BACK ROOM DEALS WITH MAJOR CORPORATIONS AND OTHER BUSINESS LEADERS. WE KNOW IT TAKES MONEY TO RUN A SUCCESSFUL CAMPAIGN. ONCE IN OFFICE THESE ELECTED OFFICIALS OFTEN DISAPPOINT US BECAUSE WE FAIL TO UNDERSTAND WHERE THEIR REAL LOYALTY LIES. WE KNOW THAT MONEY PAYS THE BILLS AND POLITICAL CONTACTS CAN HELP ACHIEVE PERSONAL GOALS. YOU MUST ASK YOURSELF, WHERE DOES THIS LEAVE ME, THE VOTER.

IF WE ARE TO DEMAND BETTER REPRESENTATION FROM OUR ELECTED OFFICIALS THEN WE MUST DO BETTER RESEARCH INTO WHO BACKS THEM FINANCIALLY. IF I PAID YOUR BILLS AND COULD FURTHER YOUR CAREER WHAT WOULD I MEAN TO YOU.

IGNITE

MIGHT HEIGHT, FIGHT RIGHT, IGNITE LIGHT, SIGHT DELIGHT, PLIGHT UNITE, DESPITE WHITE, DYNO MIGHT.

DIVINE INTERVENTION

THE UNIVERSAL PROGRESSION OF SUPREME INTELLIGENCE KNOWS WHEN DIVINE INTERVENTION IS A MUST. THE DIVINE MIND OF OUR CREATOR SPEAKS TO US THROUGH OUR SPIRITS AND PROVIDES FOR US A GUIDANCE WHEN OBEYED WILL PRODUCE FOR US THE LOVE, PEACE, JOY, HARMONY AND PROSPERITY WITH WHICH WE SEEK TO FILL OUR DAILY LIVES. BEING IN ONENESS WITH THE DIVINE MIND OF OUR CREATOR WILL ESTABLISH A FRIENDSHIP WHICH AT TIMES WILL BE BEYOND OUR HUMAN COMPREHENSION. ALWAYS SEEK TO BUILD ON THIS FRIENDSHIP AND ALWAYS MAINTAIN A STRONG LINE OF COMMUNICATION WITH THIS DIVINE MIND.

AS OUR DIVINE EVOLUTION CONTINUES ITS PROCESS LET US CONTINUE BEING THANKFUL FOR THE LOVE WE KNOW. LET'S GIVE HONOR TO THE BEAUTIFUL SPIRITS THAT CONNECTS US TO OUR PAST, THE SPIRITS THAT PROTECT US IN OUR PRESENCE AND THE SPIRITS THAT GUIDES US TO THE ONENESS WITHIN CREATION.

LET'S HUMBLY SEEK ONENESS WITH THE LIGHT AND GUIDANCE FROM THE DIVINE MIND OF OUR BELOVED CREATOR.

WE ARE HERE IN PROCESS, WE WERE CREATED FOR A DIVINE PURPOSE, WE ARE GUIDED BY A DIVINE MIND TO PROSPER.

IN THE WAY

THE REASON WE CANNOT IDENTIFY WITH OUR TRUE SELF IS BECAUSE OUR THOUGHTS AND ACTIONS ARE OUT OF ORDER. WE ARE TOO BUSY TEXTING. WE WILL TEXT FOR HOURS YET FIND IT DIFFICULT TO USE THAT SAME DEVICE TO LEARN WITH FOR FIFTEEN MINUTES.

IF YOU ARE WASTING YOUR TIME DOING NOTHING PRODUCTIVE FOR YOURSELF THEN YOU ARE IN THE WAY. YOU ARE AMONG THE LIVING, BUT YOUR LIVING IS DEAD,

VALUE OF LOVE

OUR VALUE OF LOVE IS OFTEN EQUATED WITH THE PHYSICAL PRESENCE OF MATERIAL. WE CANNOT DENY THAT THE SENSUAL AND SATISFYING ACTIONS OF SEXUAL INTERCOURSE PRODUCES A WONDERFUL EXPERIENCE OF EXPRESSION, EXPLORATION AND EXCITEMENT. HOWEVER, THE VALUE OF THE PHYSICAL IS OFTEN GIVEN MORE IMPORTANCE THAN THE VALUE OF THE MENTAL, EMOTIONAL AND SPIRITUAL ASPECTS OF OUR LIVES.

THIS VALUE SYSTEM LEAVES US UNBALANCED AND IS VERY DESTRUCTIVE TO OUR PROCESS TOWARDS PROGRESS IN PURPOSE.

THE HARMONIOUS BALANCE OF THE TRINITY, THE PHYSICAL, MENTAL, SPIRITUAL, IS EQUAL TO THE HARMONIOUS BALANCE OF OUR KNOWLEDGE, UNDERSTANDING AND WISDOM.

THE PRICELESS VALUE OF LOVE IS DIVINELY EXPERIENCED THROUGH OUR SPIRITS, AND IT IS THROUGH OUR SPIRITS OF ONENESS THAT WE MUST LEARN TO KNOW AND SHARE LOVE.

ME AND YOU

WHAT AM I DOING AND WHERE AM I GOING? HOW DO I GET THERE AND WHERE IS THE KNOWING?

EXCUSE ME MAM WOULD YOU HELP ME PLEASE? OR WILL THE ANSWER COME WHEN I'M ON MY KNEES?

I AM SEARCHING FOR THE ANSWERS THAT MUST COME, I REFUSE TO LIVE MY LIFE AS A HOMELESS WORTHLESS BUM.

I AM POWERFUL, I AM GREAT, I AM DIVINE. I WILL THROW AWAY THIS DOPE, I WILL POUR OUT THIS WINE.

I HAVE A PURPOSE IN THIS WORLD AND THIS YOU WILL SEE. A PURPOSE THAT WITH TIME I WILL TRULY COME TO BE.

WHEN YOU LOOK AT SOMEONE'S PAIN DO YOU SEE YOUR OWN? WHEN YOUR HEART CRIES INSIDE DO YOU MAKE IT KNOWN? WE WILL STRUGGLE IN THIS LIFE, BUT WE WILL MAKE IT THROUGH JUST REACH OUT AND HELP SOMEONE, BECAUSE ONE DAY THAT SOMEONE MAYBE YOU.

HUMANITY

WHY ARE WE LOSING OUR HUMANITY?

LOOK AT THE DIRECTION IN WHICH THE MAJORITY OF US ARE HEADED AND WE WILL SEE THAT MANY PEOPLE TODAY DO NOT ACKNOWLEDGE THE GOD GIVEN SPIRIT RESIDING IN EVERY HUMAN BEING. IN TODAY'S COMMUNITIES A SIMPLE HELLO TO A SPIRIT THAT ONE IS UNFAMILIAR WITH IS VERY HARD TO RECEIVE. WHILE FAMILIARITY IS ESSENTIAL IN ESTABLISHING A PHYSICAL RELATIONSHIP WE MUST UNDERSTAND THAT THE ESSENCE IN WHICH WE LIVE AND BREATHE IS ONE AND THE SAME AND THIS RELATIONSHIP HAS BEEN ONGOING SINCE THE BEGINNING OF CREATION.

WE SEE THE ECONOMICAL EXPLOITATION OF KEMET (AFRIKKKA) AND IT'S NATURAL RESOURCES AND FAIL TO MAKE THE CONNECTION. WE SEE THE INCREASE IN THE PRISON POPULATION AND FAIL TO MAKE THE CONNECTION. WE SEE THE SCIENTIFIC CREATION OF AIDS, BIRD FLU, MAD COW, SWINE FLU AND COVID 19 AND FAIL TO MAKE THE CONNECTION. WE OFTEN MAKE THE CONNECTION WHEN ONE OF OUR LOVE ONES SUDDENLY CONTRACT HIV, MAD COW, SWINE FLU OR COVID 19.

WE HAVE YET TO FULLY UNDERSTAND THAT WHEN OUR NEIGHBOR SUFFER, WE ALSO SUFFER. WE FAIL TO UNDERSTAND THAT WHEN A FAMILY MEMBER IS SENT TO PRISON THE ENTIRE FAMILY WILL SUFFER A FORM OF INCARCERATION. WE FAIL TO UNDERSTAND THAT WHEN A LOVED ONE CONTRACTS A DEADLY DIS-EASE THE ENTIRE FAMILY WILL BE AFFECTED.

IN LOSING OUR HUMANITY WE TEND TO ASS-U-ME THAT THE PLACE AND DISTANCE OF AN EVENT DETERMINES WHETHER OR NOT WE WILL BE AFFECTED. BY UNDERSTANDING OUR HUMANITY WE MUST UNDERSTAND THE DIVINE PRINCIPLES OF ONENESS. THE DIVINE PRINCIPLES OF ONENESS IS AN EXPOSITION OF THE RELATIONSHIPS (COMPLIMENTARY, SUPPLEMENTARY, INTERDEPENDENCE, ETC.) THAT EACH THING IN THE WORLD HAS WITH ALL OTHERS AND TO THE WHOLE.

WHAT YOU THINK SAY AND DO WILL AFFECT SOMEONE IN A POSITIVE OR A NEGATIVE MANNER. IN TURN THEIR POSITIVE OR NEGATIVE ENCOUNTER WITH YOU WILL HAVE AN AFFECT ON HOW THEY INTERACT

WITH THE NEXT HUMAN THEY ENCOUNTER. WITHIN ALL OF HUMANITY THERE IS A DIVINE ENERGY THAT CONNECTS US TO THE ONENESS OF OUR CREATOR AND ALL OF CREATION. THIS ENERGY WILL PRODUCE BOTH POSITIVE AND NEGATIVE FORCES, IT'S CHOICE OF PRODUCTION WILL BE DETERMINED BY WHAT WE THINK, SAY AND DO BOTH TO OURSELVES AND TO OTHERS.

HOW CAN WE HAVE PEACE IN OUR PHYSICAL WORLD WHEN WE DON'T HAVE PEACE IN OUR MENTAL AND SPIRITUAL WORLD? HOW CAN WE ENCOURAGE AND UPLIFT SOMEONE WHEN OUR WORDS ARE OFTEN DISCOURAGING AND DEGRADING? AND HOW CAN WE EXPECT TO PRODUCE A BETTER WORLD WHEN WE OFTEN COMPLAIN ABOUT THE PROBLEM YET FAIL TO IMPLEMENT A SOLUTION.

WE ARE LOSING OUR HUMANITY BECAUSE WE LOST KNOWLEDGE OF OUR TRUE IDENTITY. WE OFTEN IDENTIFY OURSELVES IN THE PHYSICAL INSTEAD OF THE SPIRITUAL. IN THE SPIRITUAL WORLD WE WILL KNOW THAT THERE IS NO ME WITHOUT YOU. IN THE SPIRITUAL WORLD WE WILL KNOW THAT THE ESSENCE OF CREATION IS A DIVINE ENERGY THAT CONNECTS US TO ALL CREATURES IN CREATION. IN THE SPIRITUAL WORLD WE KNOW THAT THERE IS A HARMONIOUS BALANCE CREATIVELY CREATED WITHIN EVERYTHING IN CREATION. IN THE SPIRIT OF ONENESS WE KNOW THAT THE ESSENCE OF HUMANITY IS THE DIVINE ENERGY THAT CONNECTS US TO OUR BELOVED CREATOR. WHEN WE COME TO KNOW, LOVE AND UNDERSTAND THIS DIVINE ENERGY WE WILL KNOW TO LOVE AND UNDERSTAND OUR BROTHERS AND SISTERS. WE WILL KNOW MY PROSPERITY IS YOUR PROSPERITY AND MY OPPRESSION IS YOUR OPPRESSION. WE WILL UNDERSTAND THE WISDOM OF OUR ANCIENT AND RECENT ANCESTORS WHO UNDERSTOOD THAT IT TAKES A VILLAGE TO RAISE A CHILD. WE WILL UNDERSTAND THAT YOUR PAIN IS MY PAIN AND THAT WITH A LITTLE HELP AND A LITTLE LOVE WE CAN BRING JOY AND REMOVE THE PAIN.

LET'S CRITICALLY ANALYZE OUR THOUGHTS, ACTIONS AND MORAL VALUES, AND WHEN WE GET DONE, LET'S DO IT AGAIN. IN THESE DAYS IT IS OF UTMOST IMPORTANCE THAT WE PRODUCE THE ATMOSPHERE IN WHICH WE DESIRE TO CREATE FOR HUMANITY. WE ARE LOSING OUR HUMANITY BECAUSE WE EXPECT TO BE LOVED BY OTHERS YET WE PRODUCE SO MUCH HATRED AND EVIL. AND IF YOU ARE NOT PRODUCING EVIL AND HATRED YOU ARE AFRAID TO STAND UP AND COURAGEOUSLY REPRESENT YOUR TRUE HUMAN SPIRIT.

ALWAYS KEEP IN MIND THAT THE ENERGY THAT YOU PRODUCE WILL REMAIN PRESENT IN THE ATMOSPHERE OF THE UNIVERSE. IF YOU DESIRE TO BE TREATED AND RESPECTED AS A HUMAN BEING THEN PLEASE DO THE SAME TO YOUR FELLOW HUMANS. LOVE ME AS YOU LOVE YOURSELF AND LET'S VALUE THE DIVINE SPIRIT WITHIN EVERYONE WE SEE.

BLACK ON BLACK RACISM

WE WILL OFTEN HEAR A BLACK PERSON CRY OUT RACISM WHEN A WHITE PERSON DOES SOMETHING SPECIAL FOR ANOTHER WHITE PERSON. WE WILL OFTEN HEAR THIS PERSON SAY THAT THEY ARE NOT PREJUDICE AND THAT ALL PEOPLE SHOULD BE TREATED THE SAME. THEY WILL OFTEN SAY THAT WE ARE ALL CHILDREN OF THE MOST HIGH GOD AND WE ALL WERE MADE PERFECT IN HIS IMAGE.

HIS-STORY IS ONLY A REMINDER OF WHAT IS GOING ON IN THIS WORLD TODAY. LOOK AT THE PRISON SYSTEM AND YOU WILL SEE RACISM. LOOK AT THE EDUCATION SYSTEM AND YOU WILL SEE RACISM. LOOK AT THE RELIGIOUS INSTITUTIONS AND YOU WILL SEE RACISM. LOOK AT THE EMPLOYMENT SYSTEM AND YOU WILL SEE RACISM. LOOK AT THE HEALTH SYSTEM AND YOU WILL SEE RACISM. LOOK AT THE POLITICAL SYSTEM AND YOU WILL SEE RACISM.

WHEN YOU CRITICALLY ANALYZE HIS-STORY AND EXAM IT'S PAST AND PRESENT POLITICAL AGENDA YOU WILL SEE AND UNDERSTAND THE SOPHISTICATION OF THE RACIST AGENDA BEING IMPLEMENTED IN TODAY'S SOCIETY.

WHEN WE LOOK AT A SO-CALLED RACIST WE WILL OFTEN SEE A PERSON WHO HAS A SUBSTANTIAL AMOUNT OF LOVE FOR HIS OR HER OWN RACE. THIS PERSON OFTEN UNDERSTANDS THAT CHARITY STARTS AT HOME AND IF HIS OR HER RACE IS TO BE LOVED AND RESPECTED BY OTHERS THEN THIS LOVE AND RESPECT MUST COME FROM WITHIN THE RACE BEFORE IT COULD TRULY BE SHARED WITH OTHERS. IN THIS SENSE A RACIST CREATES THE ENVIRONMENT THAT WILL SERVE THE BEST INTEREST OF HIS PEOPLE. THE RACISM THAT HURTS KEMETIANS, TODAY, (AFRICA IS THE NAME OF A WHITE MAN, KEMET IS THE ORIGINAL NAME OF THE LAND), IS BLACK ON BLACK RACISM. BLACKS ARE OFTEN TRAINED (NOT TAUGHT) TO BELIEVE THAT EVERYBODY SHOULD BE TREATED EQUAL. IN A PERFECT WORLD THIS WOULD BE A PERFECT SOLUTION ADHERED TO BY PERFECT PEOPLE.

WHILE MANY BLACK PEOPLE ARE BEGINNING TO SEE WITH THEIR THIRD EYE, TOO MANY OF US FAIL TO UNDERSTAND THAT IF WE DON'T MAKE IT OUR DUTY TO TAKE CARE OF ONE ANOTHER, THEN WHO WILL?

WHY SHOULD WE EXPECT ANYONE FROM ANY RACE TO DO ANYTHING OF VALUE FOR US WHEN WE DON'T REALIZE THAT WE ARE SPECIAL?

WHEN A WHITE PERSON SEE ANOTHER WHITE PERSON THEY OFTEN SEE THEMSELVES OR A VERY CLOSE FAMILY MEMBER. WHEN A SPECIAL FAVOR IS DONE IT IS DONE IN THE BEST INTEREST OF THE FAMILY.

UNCONDITIONAL LOVE AND UNDERSTANDING STARTS AT HOME BLACK PEOPLE, AND IF WE REFUSE TO SHARE DIVINE LOVE AND UNDERSTANDING WITHIN OUR OWN FAMILY WHY SHOULD WE EXPECT TO RECEIVE ANY FORM OF LOVE OR RESPECT FROM ANY OTHER RACE. STOP COMPLAINING ABOUT THE LOVE THAT THE WHITE RACE SHARES AMONGST IT'S PEOPLE, IT IS ONLY RIGHT THAT THEY TAKE CARE OF THEIR OWN. THE PROBLEM WITH BLACK PEOPLE ISN'T WHAT THE WHITE RACE IS DOING FOR THEMSELVES BUT WHAT WE ARE NOT DOING FOR EACH OTHER. THE BLAME GAME IS OVER BLACK PEOPLE WE ARE THE PROBLEM, HOWEVER, WE ARE ALSO THE SOLUTION. ACCEPT RESPONSE-ABILITY FOR BEING A LIGHT IN YOUR ENVIRONMENT AND LEARN TO LOVE AND SHARE LOVE WITH YOUR BLACK FAMILY.

AM I A LIE?

AM I A LIE? THEN WHY DO I CRY? LOOK INTO MY EYE, I DON'T WANNA DIE.

HOW DO I BECOME THE REAL ME? HOW DO I LIVE FOR OTHERS AND STILL BE FREE?

DO YOU REALLY KNOW?

DO YOU REALLY KNOW WHAT YOU KNOW? DO YOU REALLY KNOW HOW TO GROW?

DO YOU REALLY KNOW HOW LONG YOU'RE GONNA LIVE? DO YOU REALLY KNOW HOW MUCH TO GIVE?

DO YOU REALLY KNOW HOW THE UNIVERSE WAS MADE? DO YOU REALLY KNOW HOW THE FOUNDATION WAS LAID?

DO YOU REALLY KNOW WHY YOU DO THE THINGS YOU DO? DO YOU REALLY KNOW IF WHAT THE PREACHER SAYS IS TRUE?

DO YOU REALLY KNOW IF THERE IS A HEAVEN? DO YOU REALLY KNOW IF FOUR PLUS FOUR IS REALLY SEVEN?

DO YOU KNOW IF WRONG IS REALLY RIGHT? DO YOU REALLY KNOW WHO IS THE LIGHT?

DO YOU REALLY KNOW THAT THE ANSWER TO THESE QUESTIONS ISN'T VERY FAR? JUST LOOK WITHIN YOURSELF AND TRUST WHAT YOU FIND, WITHIN YOU IS THE LIGHT, YOUR GUIDING STAR.

DEAR GOD

DEAR GOD,

SOMETIMES I DON'T KNOW IF YOU'RE REALLY THERE FOR ME. I TRY TO MAINTAIN A POSITIVE OUTLOOK, BUT NEGATIVITY ALWAYS SEEMS TO BE A PART OF MY PROCESS. I KNOW THAT THINGS WON'T BE ALL GOOD ALL THE TIMES, BUT MAN, WHERE IS THE BALANCE? IT SEEMS LIKE I WILL TAKE TWO STEPS FORWARD ONLY TO TAKE TEN STEPS BACKWARDS.

GOD!!!

ARE YOU REALLY THERE? DO YOU REALLY CARE?

DEAR VINCENT,

I LOVE YOU MY SUN. I PUT YOU THROUGH THOSE THINGS BECAUSE I KNOW YOU COULD HANDLE THEM. WHEN YOU TAKE THEM TWO STEPS FORWARD I AM THERE AND WHEN YOU TAKE TEN STEP BACKWARDS I AM ALSO THERE. SOMETIMES I NEED TO SLOW YOU DOWN BECAUSE YOU ARE ABOUT TO WRECK AND I NEED TO REACH AND TEACH YOU.

VINCENT, WE ARE FRIENDS, SO I DON'T MIND THE QUESTIONS. MY REQUEST TO YOU IS THAT YOU SHARE MORE OF YOUR TIME WITH ME, LEARN AS MUCH AS YOU CAN ABOUT ME AND ALLOW ME TO GUIDE YOUR THOUGHTS, ACTIONS AND DEEDS. AND VINCENT, ALWAYS REMEMBER THAT I AM THE LIGHT THAT MAKES YOU SHINE. AND YES, I AM HERE AND YES, I REALLY DO CARE.

DEAR GOD,

THANK YOU FOR YOUR QUICK RESPONSE AND YOUR DIVINE UNDERSTANDING. MY HEART KNOWS THAT YOU LOVE ME AND I ALSO KNOW THAT YOU ARE ALWAYS HERE FOR ME. PLEASE FORGIVE ME FOR MY MOMENTS OF DOUBTS AND CONFUSION. I LOVE YOU MY GOD, AND I THANK YOU FOR LOVING ME. PLEASE CONTINUE GUIDING ME WITH YOUR TENDER MERCIES AND LOVING KINDNESS. ASHAY.

GIVING THANKS

GOD MUST BE THANKED AND PRAISED FOR GUIDING AND PROTECTING ME MENTALLY, PHYSICALLY, EMOTIONALLY AND SPIRITUALLY THROUGH 26 YEARS OF INCARCERATION. THE FOUNDATION OF WHO I AM TODAY IS FIRMLY BASED ON THIS RELATIONSHIP AND I WILL FOREVER SEEK AND TRUST THE GUIDANCE FROM OUR BELOVED CREATOR.

AT THE COMPLETION OF THIS BOOK I HAVE BEEN LIVING IN DANGRIGA, BELIZE FOR ALMOST TWO YEARS. GETTING ACCLIMATED TO A DIFFERENT CULTURE, MEANS GETTING ACCLIMATED TO NEW AND DIFFERENT CULTURAL MORALS AND VALUES THAT HAS SOMETIMES BEEN DIFFICULT, FOR THEIR UNCONDITIONAL SUPPORT I GIVE THANKS TO MRS. VERNA FIGUEROA, VANAE PATTON, FAUSTINO GAMBOA JR. MS. GEORGETTE LAMBEY, MS. ERROLYN MURRAY, ELAINE LAMBEY, JOYCE CAYETANO, MARIE LAMBEY, ROSE LAMBEY, YVONNE MCFADZEAN). DALTON GAMBOA, STANLEY LAMBEY, MRS. CECILIA ARANDA, CAROLYN HIGINIO, ALBERTA HIGINIO, MS. CAROL MEDINA, MS. STELLA HAIOULANI, MS. MONA BROWN. MR. JAMES GAMBOA JR. MR. JAHI MOODY, DEMETRIUS WESLEY ALTON PALACIO & VICKIE, GEORGE MOSS, EMERSON CACHO & DAISEY, GARRETE SUTHERLAND, HEAD RAS MALLEY, LYMPA, KENROD AND MR. ANTHONY BRANCH. FOR THOSE NOT MENTIONED PLEASE KNOW THAT YOUR LOVE IS ALWAYS APPRECIATED.

AND MY PRISON FAMILY, SPEEDY (DLB), WESLEY-BEY, OG RUMBLE (PPB)OG STEIN (69ECC), OG KD, OG K.B,, OG SLIM, OG KENDOGG OG FREDDOGG, (200LS) OG TERMITE OG LIL KURKIE (30 PIRU) THANK Y'ALL FOR HAVING MY BACK AND GIVING ME WISDOM WHEN I NEEDED IT. PLEASE KNOW THAT I WILL NEVER FORGET WHERE I CAME FROM, PLEASE KEEP ME IN YOUR PRAYERS AND KNOW THAT MY SUCCESS IS YOUR SUCCESS.

TO MY ANCESTORS PERCY & LUISA HIGINIO, FAUSTINO & SEFERINA GAMBOA, ALICE & JUAN PABLO LAMBEY, CELIA FLORES, RAYMOND GAMBOA, RICHARD HIGINIO, BERNARD HIGINIO, PETER GAMBOA, DENMARK LINO, WAYMAN MOORE, NAT TURNER, MARCUS GARVEY, BOB MARLEY, JESUS THE CHRIST, HAILE SELASSIE I, QUEENIE CHARLOTTE FLORES, ANDREW MARIN, RAFER RHODES, OG GOLDIE, OG JESSE JAMES, MARK HIGINIO, OG CHAMP, NELSON MANDELA, JOHN LEWIS, JOHN PAUL LAMBEY, (TOO TOO TOO MANY TO MENTION) I THANK YOU FOR YOUR UNCONDITIONAL LOVE, SACRIFICES AND GUIDING SPIRITS. I LOVE YOU.

TO THE READER THANK YOU FOR YOUR TIME AND SUPPORT. THE PROCEEDS FROM THIS BOOK WILL BE INVESTED IN MY CLOTHING LINE ENERGYWEBE FASHIONS. YOU CAN LEARN MORE ABOUT ME AND THE PROJECTS I AM WORKING ON BY CONTACTING ME ON FACEBOOK @ VINCENT HIGINIO OR EMAIL ME AT VINCENTHIGINIO275@GMAIL.COM.

NOW THAT I AM OUT OF PRISON, I MUST FULFILL MY VISION.

OUR CREATOR CREATED US TO CREATIVELY CREATE OUR OWN CREATION, PEACEFUL
PURPOSE-FILLED PROSPEROUS PRODUCTION MUST BE OUR PREPARATION.

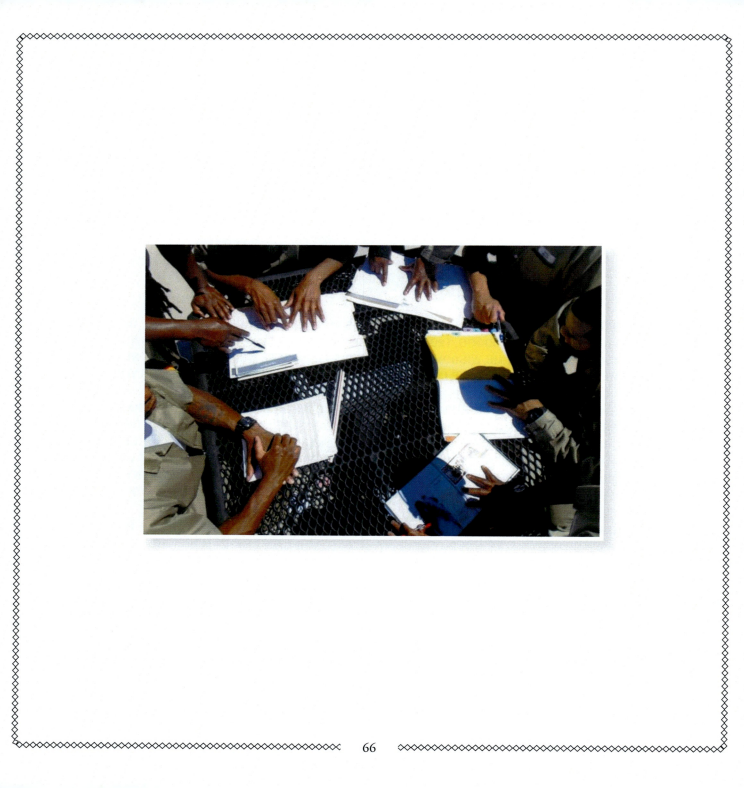

FAITH
FORWARDS
FINANCIAL
FREEDOM
FOR
FABULOUSFUTURE
FOR
FAMILY&FRIENDS

Printed in the United States
by Baker & Taylor Publisher Services